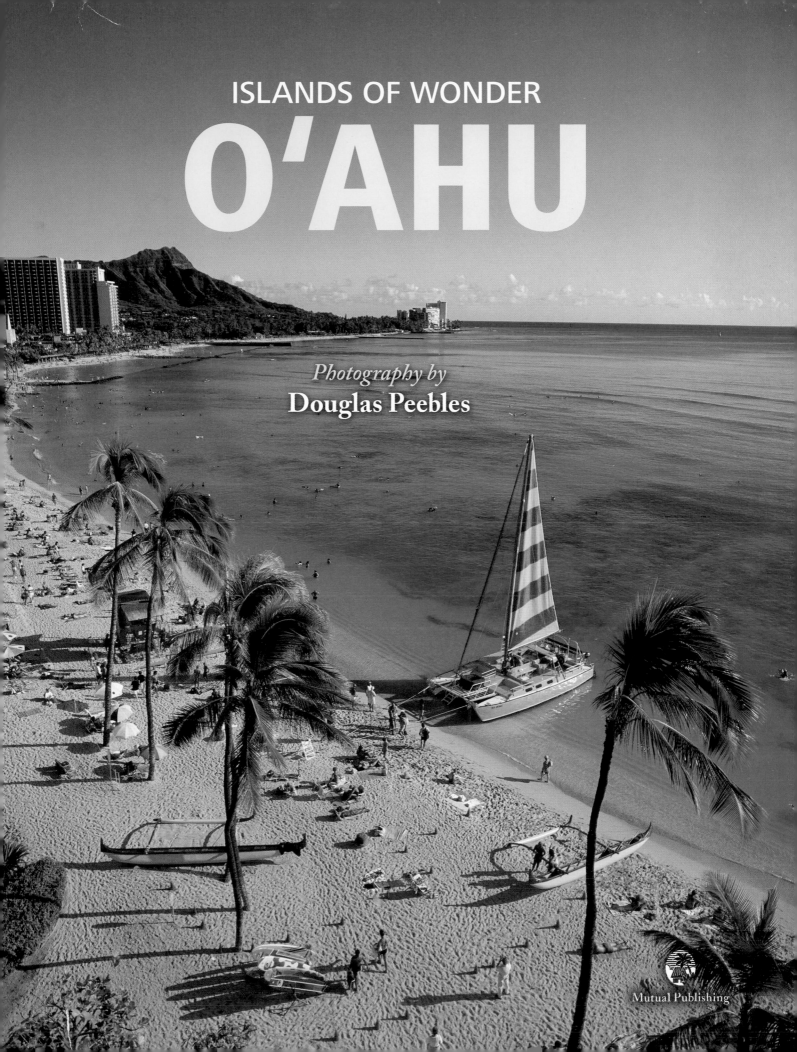

ISLANDS OF WONDER
O'AHU

Photography by
Douglas Peebles

Mutual Publishing

Cultural editors: Manu Boyd and Kainoa Daines
Library of Congress Control Number: 2014947156
ISBN: 978-1-939487-32-2

First Printing, November 2014

Mutual Publishing, LLC
1215 Center Street, Suite 210
Honolulu, Hawai'i 96816
Ph: 808-732-1709 / Fax: 808-734-4094
email: info@mutualpublishing.com
www.mutualpublishing.com

Printed in China

Preceeding page: Tourmaline blue waters, brightly colored catamarans, and the familiar silhouette of Diamond Head identify Waikīkī, the most famous resort and recreation spot in the world, with its expansive, shallow bay edging along the beach's curvature. Waikīkī means "spouting waters," in reference to the duck ponds, taro fields, and swamps that once filled most of it.

Diamond Head was originally known as Lēʻahi, meaning "brow of the tuna" referring to the crater's profile. It is Hawaiʻi's most famous landmark, rising 760 feet to provide a dramatic backdrop for Waikīkī. Its eroded crater walls form a perfectly round tuff cone. Tuff is a relatively soft rock composed of cemented ash and stone particles created by a sudden explosive eruption in which magma comes in contact with water, creating steam. Diamond Head was formed over 300,000 years ago during a single brief, steam-fueled eruption when seawater came into contact with lava seeping out of a fissure.

Diamond Head has inspired voyagers, artists, poets, songwriters, naturalists, and hikers. It was once speckled with calcite crystals mistaken by early sailors for diamonds, hence the name Diamond Head.

This late-afternoon scene encompasses most of what Waikīkī is famous for—its swaying coconut palms, blue placid water, and sandy beaches. Waikīkī is Hawai'i's urban paradise and favorite playground, attracting surfers, swimmers, paddlers, kayakers, sunbathers, people-watchers, joggers, and volleyball players.

INTRODUCTION

Welcome to the island of O'ahu, where Polynesia meets the twenty-first century—and both win. Nowhere in Hawai'i are the contemporary realities and complexities of life in paradise more vivid: the booming prosperity, the cultural and ethnic confluences, the proud history, the trade-offs between preservation and progress—all played out against a spectacular natural beauty.

The simplest images express it best: Honolulu's glittering high-rises crowded between a blue sea and emerald mountains; freeway traffic cooled by soft trade winds and gilded by blazing sunsets; the stunning regularity of rainbows arched over both the city and its outlying plains.

Honolulu and its Waikīkī resort district usually overwhelm any other impression of the island. However, the great surprise to most visitors is how spectacular the rest of O'ahu is, both physically and socially. Topographically, O'ahu's 600-square mile, mature volcanic island is the most varied and intimate of the major Hawaiian Islands. Spread out along O'ahu's four distinct coastlines, like a dreamer's checklist of tropical essentials, are coral reefs, sheltered lagoons, wide beaches, broad, well-defined bays, view-perfect promontories, mist-shrouded valleys, dry leeward plains, and sheer velvet cliffs.

The long Ko'olau Mountain Range to the east and the Wai'anae Mountain Range to the west, with a broad central plain in between, define the island. The peaks, rising to 4,000 feet, sloping ridges, and steep-walled pali (cliffs) are the remains of the much higher Ko'olau and Wai'anae volcanoes that emerged from the Pacific about 3 million years ago. On O'ahu, nature has had plenty of time to rearrange its crude volcanoes into a magical landscape. Eons of stream and wave erosion have carried much of the original mass back into the sea, leaving behind the soft, deeply folded draperies of Windward O'ahu and the alternating valleys and ridges that provide Honolulu's

continued on page 7

dramatic backdrop. Later volcanic activity added the finishing touch with a series of volcanic cones—the beloved landmarks of Diamond Head, Punchbowl, and Koko Head.

O'ahu has been known as "the gathering place" since ancient days when chiefs from the other islands conferred at Waikīkī, which was then neutral ground. Its modern history begins in late 1794 when the British fur trading ship, *Jackal*, inched through a break in the coral reef protecting what was then the small O'ahu fishing village of Kou and found a commodious harbor that the sailors named Fair Haven—later to be named Honolulu, meaning "protected bay." The promise of a safe anchorage and nearby fresh water and food (and, no doubt, its exotic name) drew adventurers, sandalwood traders, merchants, and whalers from America and Europe. By 1850, when the royal capital was relocated here from Lahaina, Maui, Honolulu was a bustling Pacific port of call.

Today, the island has almost a million residents, representing 70 percent of Hawai'i's population. On any given day it hosts about 100,000 visitors. Honolulu is the state capital and the headquarters for all economic activity. The U.S. Army, Navy, and Air Force commands based on O'ahu involve 110,000 military personnel and their dependents.

The City and County of Honolulu—a single political entity—covers the entire island; "Honolulu" usually refers to the urban swatch along O'ahu's south shore from Koko Head in the east to Pearl Harbor in the west, and from the ocean into the Ko'olau Mountain Range.

O'ahu's pleasures are the same today as yesterday. The trade winds continue to blow and the pure colors of the mountains and the sea continue to amaze. Honolulu is still, by any measure, a glamorous, glorious city. Every day its golden people prove the remarkable durability of the aloha spirit, the guileless local friendliness that transcends the realities of the twenty-first century.

One way to relax in Waikīkī is to lounge just above the ocean's edge in an infinity pool filled with adult-sized floating beanbags as coconut palms sway overhead.

The shallow, reef-protected waters and white sand beaches of Waikīkī are an ocean wonderland. Surfers, snorkelers, and boogie boarders can delight in a tropical water playground as Waikīkī's light waves and clear waters make for easy and safe water sports. Catamaran rides and sail tours are offered daily to explore and enjoy the offshore waters.

Because of its clear water, rolling waves, and constant sunshine, Waikīkī has always been a popular surfing spot. In the days when Waikīkī was the playground of Hawaiian royalty, the ali'i (chiefs) often rode the waves here, and a nearby heiau on the slopes of Diamond Head was dedicated to the sport.

By the early 1900s, surfing had nearly died out in Waikīkī when a group of revivalists—including the world-famous beachboy, Duke Kahanamoku—attracted renewed interest in the sport. Today, on any given day, Waikīkī's waters are filled with surfers.

Breaking from 2 to 8 feet, the waves in many spots are perfect for beginners, with rides sometimes extending for more than a hundred yards. There are at least sixteen identifiable surf spots in the Waikīkī–Diamond Head area.

In the shadow of Diamond Head Crater lies Queen Kapi'olani Regional Park, a gathering place within walking distance of Waikīkī's hotels. On evenings and weekends, the park fills for family events and recreational activities. During daytime and weekdays, there is a stream of joggers and strollers, yoga classes, and soccer practices. The 170 acres of greenery were dedicated as a park on June 11, 1877, by King Kalākaua in honor of his wife, Queen Kapi'olani. Through its history, it has served as a polo field, a racetrack, and an army post.

In ancient times, the hula with accompanying mele or chants, was a sacred form of storytelling, a means of recording and passing on historic events, legendary tales, and the accomplishments of brave warriors or aliʻi (chiefs). Today both its traditional and modern forms are celebrated and performed at private and public gatherings, hotel venues, and competitions. The world-renowned Merrie Monarch Festival is held in April of every year, attracting hālau (dance troupes) from all the islands, as well as the U.S. mainland and Japan.

Hawaiian music actually consists of several different styles, from ancient chanting to crossovers with reggae rhythms. In Waikīkī you can hear traditional music, nostalgic tunes of the 1940s and 1950s, and sophisticated jazz stylings with a tropical flare.

The Royal Hawaiian Center, in Waikīkī's center, offers complimentary hula shows and Hawaiian music. Many brand-name stores are found here, as well as dozens of excellent fine-dining restaurants to choose from after the day's excursions. This site, known as Helumoa, was once the royal residence of Princess Bernice Pauahi Bishop, the great-granddaughter of King Kamehameha I. The Princess' statue sits elegantly in the Royal Grove. Her beach cottage was located approximately at the makai end of the Royal Hawaiian Hotel lobby.

Opposite page: Hula at the water's edge can be enjoyed with an evening view of Lēʻahi (Diamond Head) in the background.

Waikīkī takes on a magic serene feel at nighttime offering a sharp contrast to daytime when the beach is blanketed with beach towels and sunbathers. When the sun goes down, there are evening shopping and dining options along Beach Walk and at the Royal Hawaiian Center.

Honolulu enjoys fireworks every July 4, New Year's Eve, and every Friday night from the Hilton Hawaiian Village in Waikīkī. One of the biggest displays is by Nagaoka Fireworks from Niigata, Japan, during the Honolulu Festival. The Nagaoka Fireworks display aims to promote world peace.
Photo © Brad Peebles

Twilight can be enjoyed at Magic Island, a few minutes walk away from Waikīkī. The colors of the aftermath of a Waikīkī sunset are unique, encompassing the hues of the sky and clouds, coconut palms, the light bouncing off sand and reflecting from the ocean water and buildings in foreground. Magic Island is a man-made peninsula completed in 1964, originally intended as a resort-to-hotel complex.

There is no substitute for the glow of a Hawai'i sunset. Flaming orange displays are an almost nightly show to be enjoyed from the cooling sands or aboard sailboat cruises. The last sliver of golden light as the sun drops beneath the horizon is the best.

This panoramic view includes Ala Moana Center, the Ala Wai Yacht Harbor, the man-made Magic Island peninsula, and the beginning of Waikīkī. Ala Moana draws more than 42 million people per year and is the world's largest open-air shopping center with 300 stores, as well as many restaurants. O'ahu's fabulous climate, multicultural lifestyles, and teeming beaches annually attract millions from around the world, reaffirming its

At the top of Lē'ahi, Diamond Head Crater, visitors pose for pictures with the breathtaking scenery of Waikīkī, the luxurious "Gold Coast" residential area, Kapi'olani Park, Honolulu's skyline, and the Wai'anae mountains in the distance. One of the newer urban O'ahu hikes is the trek to the top of Diamond Head. The 0.8-mile hike from trailhead to summit is steep, gaining 560 feet as it ascends from the crater floor. Waikīkī today, with its bustling beaches, tree-rimmed Kapi'olani Park, and densely built-up residential neighborhoods, bears little resemblance to what it was 90 years ago. Then it was composed of taro farms, rice fields, duck ponds, swamps, clusters of coconut palms behind an empty beach, a scattering of residences and weekend bungalows, and some of the world's best surfing.

Koko Head, at the southeastern end of O'ahu, is a tuff cone just inland of Hanauma Bay. It was once known as Mo'okua-o-Kāne'āpua, "the backbone of Kāne'āpua." According to legend, Kāne'āpua, the younger brother of the gods Kāne and Kanaloa, had been sent by his brothers to fetch fresh water. When he disobeyed, he was turned into this hill. (Koko Head was known earlier as 'Ihi'ihilauākea). Its crater, anciently referred to as Kohelepelepe, has a popular and strenuous hiking trail, but the views are worth the risk it takes to climb straight to the top. Both the crater and the headland take their name from a former canoe landing site nearby named Koko.

Hanauma Bay lies within a pair of volcanic craters that have been breached by the ocean. The curved beach is not very wide along its 2,000-foot length. It is internationally famous as a spectacular marine sanctuary offering a treasure trove of ocean wonders. It was formed when the seaward wall of an ancient volcanic crater collapsed. "Hanauma" has two possible meanings, one referring to the ancient sport of uma ("hand-wrestling bay") said to have been played on the beach, and "curved bay." Once a favorite retreat for Hawaiian royalty, it was also a site for scenes from the famous Elvis Presley movie, *Blue Hawaii*. Today the 101-acre expanse of crystalline blue water within this remnant of a volcanic crater is a state marine life conservation district. A protected reef teeming with unusual fishes, its crescent shores are a popular recreational spot for swimming and snorkeling. The large sand-bottom holes in the coral were the work of American GIs stationed here on beach defense during World War II. To give themselves a place to swim, the soldiers tossed grenades into the water and blew up the reef. The park's immense popularity now limits the number of visitors to protect its natural beauty and wildlife.

Makapu'u Lighthouse at the southernmost tip of O'ahu is a striking red jewel above the blue Pacific Ocean. A 2-mile round-trip hike winds its way gradually uphill past the lighthouse (which is off limits) for stunning views of the Windward coast.

Makapuʻu (bulging eye) is actually the name of the easternmost point on Oʻahu. Makapuʻu Beach is one of the best-known bodysurfing spots in the islands. It is a curved, sandy pocket about 1,000 feet long, enclosed by a high sea cliff and point of lava rock. It experiences a great deal of seasonal variation in width. During summer months the beach is wide and the ocean usually calm and safe. During the winter months, severe erosion of the beach exposes many large rocks and boulders in the shorebreak.

Seen off the shores of Makapuʻu Beach is Mānana, or Rabbit Island, a 67-acre islet. It was given its name when the owner of Waimānalo Ranch raised rabbits there as a hobby. In 1895, the island was a hiding place for weapons used in an unsuccessful attempt to restore Queen Liliʻuokalani to her throne. Today it is a state-protected seabird sanctuary.

Waimānalo (potable water), with its 5 miles of white sand and turquoise beaches, is the longest continuous sand beach on Oʻahu's southeastern side. Above the beach stand the cliffs of the Koʻolau Mountain Range in stark contrast, jutting sharply up and towering over the town below.

The views from Waimānalo of the small outlying islands and the cliffs in the background are stunning. The gently sloping ocean bottom and small waves make Waimānalo beaches perfect for family fun. The shoreline falls under two jurisdictions, each with different rules. Waimānalo Beach Park is operated by the City and County of Honolulu, as is Waimānalo Bay Recreation Center. Bellows Air Force Station opens its beach access only on weekends. All three areas offer parking.

A few years ago, this broad, 3-mile stretch of Kailua Beach on O'ahu's Windward side was the windsurfing capital of the world. Some windsurfers are still around, but most have moved to Diamond Head and Maui's north shore. Thirty-acre Kailua Beach Park, at the south end of the beach, is busy on weekends with paddle boarders and kayakers venturing the short distance to a small island bird sanctuary. Its white sands cut like a bright beam of grainy light between the bay's placid blue waters and the forest-cloaked Ko'olau Range.

The water colors here are dazzling, as is the quality of the golden sand. Waves breaking close to shore, particularly in the middle section of the beach, are great for beginning bodysurfers and body boarders. The many public rights-of way provide plenty of accessible beachfront to choose from.

Lanikai's straight, sandy, mile-long stretch of calm water was once an ancient fishing spot. Lanikai, originally known as Kaʻōhao, was recently voted one of the best beaches in the United States because of its unmatched sand, tourmaline waters, and softly sloping shoreline. Even without facilities and no nearby public parking, Lanikai lures visitors with its powdery white sands.

Developers misunderstood Hawaiian in naming Lanikai, which literally means "sea heaven," not "heavenly sea." Two offshore islands, the Mokulua ("two islands" or "double island") are protected bird sanctuaries.

The Hawaiian voyaging canoe *Hōkūle'a* eases into Kāne'ohe Bay. The *Hōkūle'a* is an accurate, full-scale replica of a Polynesian double-hulled voyaging canoe. In 1976, she voyaged from Hawai'i to Tahiti without the use of modern navigational instruments using Polynesian wayfinding techniques.

Kāneʻohe Bay is a deep lagoon protected by the only true barrier reef in Hawaiʻi. The coral reefs found here block ocean swell, creating an expanse of calm water that attracts windsurfers, sailors, paddlers, and fishermen.

The bay's 8-mile shoreline, however, has been dredged, filled, and protected with retaining walls in many places for residential development and the construction of piers. Extensive soil runoff, which for a time threatened to smother the once-spectacular reef with silt, was brought under control in the wake of citizen protests.

In ancient times, Kāneʻohe, in the shadow of the Koʻolau Mountain Range, with its beautiful sheltered bay ringed by productive fishponds and abundant coral reefs, was Oʻahu's largest population center. The Kāneʻohe Bay Sandbar—Ahualaka—is a popular recreational stop for boaters year-round.

Above: Rare small waves near Lanikai Beach (old name Ka'ōhao), give surfers a gentle ride. The calm waters here are well suited for paddleboarding and kayaking.

Left: The Kāne'ohe Bay Sandbar at high tide is a shallow submerged playground where boaters drop anchor for sunshine and water play.

Right: Looking across Kāne'ohe Bay, a ridge of the Ko'olau Mountain Range marks its northern boundary. The Kualoa land division (ahupua'a) is located at the northern end of Kāne'ohe Bay. Kualoa has great cultural significance to the Hawaiians. One of the most sacred sites on O'ahu, it was also a place of refuge in ancient times. Much of the ahupua'a is occupied today by Kualoa Ranch, owned by the Morgan family, descendants of missionaries.

Below: The Lanipō Trailtrail—a seven-mile round trip—climbs 1,600 feet to the crest of the Ko'olau Mountain Range and offers terrific views. The trailhead is next to a Board of Water Supply at the top of Wilhemina Rise.

Hawai'i's whales are part of a North Pacific humpback *(koholā)* population that migrates between Alaska and Hawai'i. Once reduced to a few hundred, this community now numbers in the low thousands, thanks to federal protection. The Hawaiian Islands Humpback Whale National Marine Sanctuary lies within the shallow (less than 600 feet), warm waters surrounding the main Hawaiian Islands and constitutes one of the world's most important humpback whale habitats. Scientists estimate that two-thirds of the entire North Pacific humpback whale population of 5,000–6,000 animals migrates to Hawaiian waters each winter to engage in breeding, calving, and nursing activities. The whales spend most of the year in Alaskan waters, feeding to prepare for the long migration south to these winter breeding grounds. Usually arriving in December but sometimes as early as November, they roam throughout the Hawaiian Island chain.

Opposite page: A pod of whales plays near Hawai'i Kai. **This page:** Here, an adult humpback breaches in the waters off Kāne'ohe Bay.

The Byodo-In Temple was built in 1968 at the Valley of the Temples Memorial Park in Kahalu'u to celebrate the 100-year anniversary of the arrival of Japanese immigrants to Hawai'i. It is a replica of the famous Kyoto Temple in Japan and houses a 3-ton bronze bell and an 18-foot-high Buddha. This popular and peaceful stop welcomes visitors of all faiths for quiet contemplation under the shadow of the Ko'olau Mountain Range.

During rainy weather, the Koʻolau Range's steep cliffs (pali) are covered with countless waterfalls. The view from the summit on a clear day overlooks the Windward side of Oʻahu and the city of Kāneʻohe. The name literally means "bamboo husband," referring to an ancient account that compared a husband's cruelty to the cutting edge of a bamboo knife.

Kaʻaʻawa Valley is north of Kāneʻohe Bay, from which it is separated by a ridge of the Koʻolau Mountain Range named Kānehoalani (left). Cattle grazing and historic taro (kalo) terraces reveal the location of a once significant village. Several blockbuster movies and television shows have been filmed near this valley on Kualoa Ranch land, including *Jurassic Park, 50 First Dates,* and *Lost.*

Kaʻaʻawa lies just beyond the valley of the same name. This view shows the uniqueness of the area's geography—mountain ridges, breaking surf, the multifaceted offshore water. Kaʻaʻawa, a small community north of Kāneʻohe Bay, is confined to a relatively narrow belt extending along the coast.

The Wahiawā fields on the Leilehua Plateau on the way to the North Shore are Oʻahu's remaining acres of pineapple. Pineapples were introduced to Hawaiʻi in the early nineteenth century but did not become a viable commercial crop until James Drummond Dole revolutionized the way that they were grown, harvested, and canned. The Dole Plantation is a popular stop when driving to Oʻahu's North Shore.

Waimea Bay is known for its huge winter waves that become a raging mass of whitewater, attracting daring surfers from all over the world. In summer, Waimea's calmer waters make it a beach for families and paddlers. Inland, one can hike to a waterfall and swimming hole at the top of nearby Waimea Botanical Gardens. Waimea means "reddish water," the result of erosion of nearby red soil. Like its namesake on Kaua'i, where Captain Cook landed in 1778, Waimea has the distinction of being the first place on O'ahu to have contact with foreigners the following year, after Cook's death at Kealakekua Bay.

The Quicksilver Big Wave International in Memory of Eddie Aikau, a Hawaiian hero and the first lifeguard at Waimea Bay, is an elite invitational surfing competition held at Waimea Bay only when wave heights reach a sustained 20 feet (30–40 foot face). Some years pass without the competition running.

Eddie Aikau was a true beachboy, a surfer through and through. He is memorialized for the heroic rescue attempt of the *Hōkūleʻa* crew that tragically led to his death in 1978.

Left: A large winter wave curls at Waimea Bay.

Below: Experienced surfers get ready to attempt the large waves.

Opposite page, top: Competitors watch the waves at Waimea Bay.
Bottom: Crowds gather on the hillside, roads, and beach of Waimea Bay during a Big Wave surfing competition.

Laniākea Beach is a popular surfing spot on O'ahu's North Shore. It is also where turtles come close into the shore to feed on the algae growing on the rock. Sometimes the turtles will haul themselves up on the beach to warm themselves and raise their body temperature by basking in the sun. Hawai'i provides feeding grounds and nesting sites for two species of sea turtle. An endangered and federally protected species, the green sea turtle, known as *honu*, is easy to observe. The much rarer hawksbill sea turtle comes to land only to lay eggs. They are smaller than green sea turtles, and younger animals have a serrated margin around the shell.

Ka'ena Point, the rugged northwesternmost point of O'ahu, is accessible only on foot. Its entire shoreline is edged by lava and reefs and has no beaches. On some days while the rain curtains to the north, the Wai'anae coast, seen to the west, is bathed in sun. Until the 1940s, trains of the O'ahu Railway and Land Co. rounded Ka'ena Point, and autos later used the abandoned roadbed to get an unparalleled view of O'ahu. Today the point is a natural area reserve off limits to vehicles. The white "golf balls" at the crest of the Wai'anae Range are plane- and satellite-tracking stations. Ka'ena means "red hot" or "glowing" because of its spectacular sunsets. In old Hawai'i, it was known as a place where souls departed earth.

Towering above the central plains of O'ahu and stretching from Ka'ena Point to 'Ewa, the Wai'anae Range is what remains of the older of two volcanoes that created the island. Kolekole Pass, the low spot in the middle of this range, marks the flight path Japanese Zeros used in their attack on Pearl Harbor.

Yokohama Beach (known to the Hawaiians as Keawa'ula) gets its name from Japanese workers of the Wai'anae Sugar Plantation who liked to fish here. Most Japanese immigrants who came to Hawai'i to work on the sugar plantation sailed out of Yokohama. It is the last sandy stretch of shore on O'ahu's northwestern coast. The beach is wide during summer. Caution must be exercised if the ocean is not completely calm.

Ocean activities dominate O'ahu's lifestyle—surfing, wind surfing, paddling, kayaking, and the latest, stand-up paddleboard surfing. The waters of Mākaha are ideal for water activities to be enjoyed against a backdrop of insurmountable beauty. "Mākaha" ("fierce" or "savage") refers to the entire valley from the mountains to the sea, including the beaches along the shoreline. The area developed as a surfing mecca after World War II.

Ulehawa Beach in Wai'anae is one of several remaining beaches on O'ahu's west coast that is less visited. The desertlike Leeward Side of O'ahu is known for its beautiful coastlines. During the summer this area is relatively calm and safe for swimming. During the winter, much of the beach disappears as the winter surf creates powerful rip currents and good bodysurfing.

The ghostly outline of the USS *Arizona* is visible beneath the 184-foot-long memorial to the 1,177 crew members who perished when the battleship was sunk during the Japanese attack on Pearl Harbor on the morning of December 7, 1941. More than 900 men are still entombed within the wreck. More than seventy years later, drops of oil from her fuel tanks—filled to the brim just before the attack—still rise as silent reminders of the gallant men below. Thousands of visitors a day are ferried by U.S. Navy personnel to view the memorial and the Wall of Names in the Shrine Room.

The Battleship USS *Missouri* Memorial, moored at Ford Island near the USS *Arizona* Memorial, is a favorite stop when visiting the historic sites at Pearl Harbor and Ford Island. Christened in the Pacific Theater in 1944, the "Mighty Mo" would go on to be the site of Japan's surrender ceremony on September 2, 1945.

Above: The USS *Bowfin* was launched on December 7, 1942, exactly one year after the attack on Pearl Harbor. A magnificent submarine that made the term "Silent Service" famous, the USS *Bowfin* was nicknamed the Pearl Harbor Avenger. She is now permanently docked at Pearl Harbor.

Right: A Japanese Zero, in mock flight preparation, can be seen at the Pacific Aviation Museum on Ford Island at Pearl Harbor.

The entrance to the USS *Missouri* is decked in American flags, cheerfully welcoming millions of visitors a year, its massive guns extending over its wooden decks.

Opposite page: The USS *Missouri's* triple 16-inch gun turret No. 1 is no longer operational. Each gun was capable of firing two 2,700-pound projectiles per minute, with a maximum range of 23 miles. A plug keeps the barrel clean and guards against accidents.

This aerial view shows part of the port of Honolulu and the city's skyline, with the Ko'olau Range in the background and Diamond Head to the right. The port of Honolulu is the entry point for almost all goods coming into Hawai'i. The busy downtown port waters of Honolulu are filled daily with giant freighters and cargo containers.

The port's history begins in late 1794 with the discovery of Honolulu's capability as a port 16 years after British Captain James Cook found and named the Sandwich Islands. A British fur trading ship, *Jackal*, inched through a break in the coral reef protecting a small O'ahu fishing village called Kou and found a commodious harbor. Honolulu, which means "protected bay" in Hawaiian, became the name for the surrounding area. The promise of a safe anchorage and nearby fresh water and food drew adventurers, sandalwood traders, merchants, and whalers from America and Europe to Honolulu. By 1850, when King Kamehameha III relocated the royal palace capital here from Lahaina, Maui, Honolulu was a bustling Pacific port-of-call.

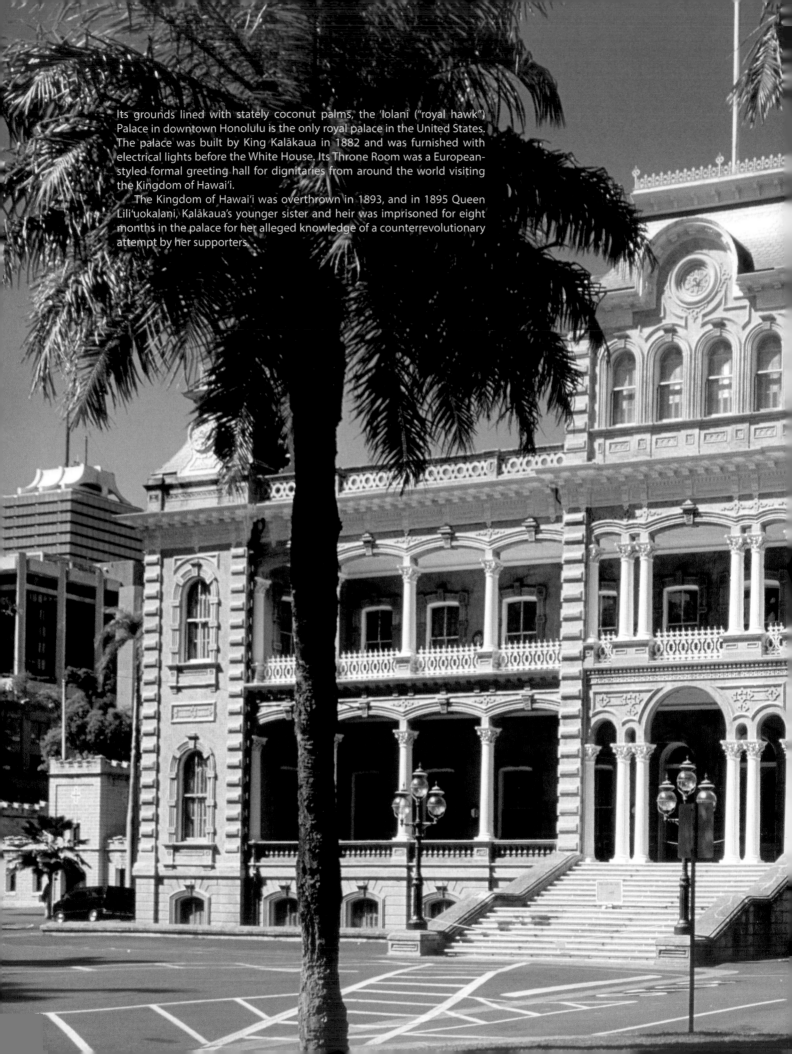

Its grounds lined with stately coconut palms, the ʻIolani ("royal hawk") Palace in downtown Honolulu is the only royal palace in the United States. The palace was built by King Kalākaua in 1882 and was furnished with electrical lights before the White House. Its Throne Room was a European-styled formal greeting hall for dignitaries from around the world visiting the Kingdom of Hawaiʻi.

The Kingdom of Hawaiʻi was overthrown in 1893, and in 1895 Queen Liliʻuokalani, Kalākaua's younger sister and heir was imprisoned for eight months in the palace for her alleged knowledge of a counterrevolutionary attempt by her supporters.

Above: Three historic structures built between 1821 and 1841 are on display at downtown Honolulu's Mission Houses Museum. The nearer house is built of coral rocks cut in Hawai'i while the farther ones are of traditional New England frame construction, and were the first Western dwellings in Hawai'i.

Right: Kawaiaha'o Church was once the chapel of Hawai'i's royal family. It was constructed between 1836 and 1842 using thousand-pound slabs of coral rock hand-chiseled from the southern waters of O'ahu, sometimes requiring divers to submerge ten feet to hammer away under water. It was the first Christian church built on the island, and services were spoken in Hawaiian up until only a few years ago.

Opposite page: The King Kamehameha Statue, commissioned by the Hawaiian Kingdom's Legislature in 1878 and cast in Paris in 1880, sank in transport off the Falkland Islands. A second arrived in Honolulu in time for King Kalākaua's coronation in 1883. It now stands in front of Hawai'i's Judiciary Building, Ali'iōlani Hale on King Street. It is adorned with lei on June 11 in honor of Kamehameha Day. The original statue now stands at Kapa'au in North Kohala on the island of Hawai'i, near the great king's birthplace.

Above: At the top of the staircase in the Court of Honor is a statue of Lady Columbia, also known as Lady Liberty, or Justice. Here she represents all grieving mothers from the bow of a ship, holding a laurel branch. The inscription below the statue, taken from President Abraham Lincoln's letter to Mrs. Bixby, reads:

THE SOLEMN PRIDE
THAT MUST BE YOURS
TO HAVE LAID
SO COSTLY A SACRIFICE
UPON THE ALTAR
OF FREEDOM

Left: Punchbowl Crater, once known to Hawaiians as Pūowaina, or "the hill for placing (of sacrifices)," is today famous as the location of the National Memorial Cemetery of the Pacific. In 1949 the bowl of this 500-foot tuff cone was dedicated as the U.S. National Memorial Cemetery of the Pacific where more than 25,000 servicemen and women, who served in World Wars I and II and the Korean and Vietnam Wars, are buried. The veterans' graves are marked by small white crosses that geometrically cover the crater's 112-acre floor during Memorial Day celebrations each year. The 26,280 fighting men listed as "missing in action" are commemorated in a "Courts of the Missing" monument on Punchbowl's interior 'Ewa slope.

The old Nu'uanu Pali Road makes its way dangerously along the cliff above the newer Pali Highway. The "Pali" is one of three highways that connects the Leeward and the Windward sides of O'ahu. Pali means cliff in Hawaiian.

Opposite page: The Nu'uanu Pali Lookout offers unparalleled views of O'ahu's Windward side from an altitude of more than a thousand feet. It provides a dramatic view of the corrugated ridges of the Ko'olau Mountain Range that rise imposingly above the natural amphitheaters below. The wind here is often strong as breezes whip up the mountainside and over the cement viewing platform causing viewers to lose hats and umbrellas.

In 1795, the famous Battle of Nu'uanu occurred here in which Kamehameha acquired the island of O'ahu in his quest for unification.

Judd Trail is a wonderful way to explore the natural beauty of Hawai'i. Starting at Nu'uanu Pali Drive, it continues until it reaches the Pali Lookout. Along the trail beautiful Hawaiian birds, plants, and flowers can be seen as one passes streams and walks through immense, beautiful forested areas. The television series *Lost* often shot in the area.

MAP OF O'AHU

WAIMEA BAY

Laniakea Beach

WAIMEA BOTANICAL GARDENS

KA'ENA POINT

Yokohama Beach

KO'OLAU MOUNTAINS

Ka'a'awa

DOLE PLANTATION

Kualoa

WAI'ANAE MOUNTAINS

MOUNT KA'ALA

KUALOA RANCH

KĀNE'OHE BAY

Mākaha Beach

BYODO-IN TEMPLE

PEARL HARBOR:
USS *ARIZONA*
USS *MISSOURI*
USS *BOWFIN*
PACIFIC AVIATION MUSEUM

Kāne'ohe

Kailua

Kailua Beach
Lanikai Beach

Ulehawa Beach

JUDD TRAIL

NU'UANU PALI

Waimanalo

Makapu'u Beach

U.S. NATIONAL MEMORIAL CEMETERY OF THE PACIFIC

DOWNTOWN HONOLULU

Waikīkī

Hawai'i Kai

KOKO HEAD

MAKAPU'U LIGHTHOUSE

HANAUMA BAY

THE HAWAIIAN ISLANDS

KAUA'I

NI'IHAU

O'AHU

MOLOKA'I

MAUI

LĀNA'I

KAHO'OLAWE

HAWAI'I